The ANUNNAKI Were Here!

(A quantum leap in the field of ancient archaeology)

By Marshall Klarfeld

Dedicated to my wife, Mary.

Mary is the best part of this book. She was responsible for editing and arranging the beautiful pictures. Without her constant "where did the water come from" questions, I would not have been able to find the extraordinary pictures that made this book possible.

Contents

Title Page
Dedication

INTRODUCTION

Throughout my life I have been fascinated by legendary structures such as the Great Pyramid at Giza, the Easter Island statues, Stonehenge and the ancient ruins at Machu Picchu. I wanted to know how they were built, who the architects were and why they were here. Every research book I have read insists these colossal creations were the work of the locals: the Egyptians, the Easter Island natives, the tribes on the Salisbury plain, the Incas, et al. It was only after my first book, ADAM, the Missing Link, that I convinced myself an advanced space age civilization, known as the ANUNNAKI, were in fact the creators of these magnificent achievements. This book will reveal my current analysis of why the ANUNNAKI invested so much time and energy in the construction of the Egyptian pyramids, Machu Picchu, Ollantaytambo, Gobekli Tepe, the Mesoamerican pyramids, Chaco Canyon and Mesa Verde.

I have always been intrigued by the constant demands of my mind when I encounter something new and interesting. It appears I have been "gifted" or "cursed" with a mind that insists I understand how things work, why they were created and what their purpose was. For example, I remember a scene years ago when I was perhaps 10 years old. My father had taken me on a trip to visit his best friend's new villa in New Hampshire. (We were living in Boston at that time.) My father's friend, Louis Puni, was a wealthy maître'D at Boston's famous Copley Plaza. Louis proudly showed me the fancy swimming pool he had just designed and built. The plumbing was a complex of pipes, valves and joints. It could have been described as a spaghetti nightmare – Louis was famous for his Italian dishes. I studied his design for several minutes and then precociously, to Louis' dismay, announced "It won't work." The plumbing was improperly connected. After further examination, Louis, somewhat angry that a 10 year old was able to discover his mistakes, agreed I was right. This day made a lasting impression on me. The manner in which my mind is able to sort out complex mechanisms has been a gift I am able to employ in my most recent research.

My last 16 years of investigating the wonders of the ANUNNAKI civilization have produced many exciting discoveries: Inca walls under the Easter Island statues, the spider's origin and the celestial map on the Nazca Lines, the 16th century painting of Cairo with many mountain tops neatly removed, the eclipse computer at Stonehenge and the apparent "branding" of many wondrous stone structures by the ANUNNAKI.

Introduction (Cont'd)

Over 300,000 cuneiform tablets, written in ancient Sumerian, have been found to date. 120,000 of these are in the British Museum. Zecharia Sitchin, a brilliant scholar and internationally renowned authority on the ANUNNAKI, deciphered 2000 of these tablets and cylinder seals. His translations describe, in great detail, the early history of the ANUNNAKI's life on our planet. Overwhelming evidence that the ANUNNAKI were here is gradually filtering through society today. It is difficult for many to believe this ancient written history because the life span of the ANUNNAKI appears to be much much longer than we can comprehend and so much of what they accomplished is beyond our current understanding.

Neil Freer, author of <u>Breaking the Godspell,</u> wrote and published in October 6, 1999 a White Paper which gives an easy to understand overview of the ANUNNAKI's history here on Earth. Here are excerpts from this White Paper.

..."The documentary evidence, i.e. the historical documentation for the existence and deeds of the Anunnaki, has been available to us since the early 1800's. The excavation of the ancient sites of Mesopotamia brought to light the amazingly advanced civilization of Sumer and, with it, thousands of clay tablets containing not only mundane records of commerce, marriages, military actions and astronomical calculation systems but of the history of the Anunnaki themselves. It is clear from these records that the Sumerians knew these aliens to be real flesh and blood. The library of the ruler, Ashurbanipal at Nineveh, was discovered to have burnt down and the clay tablets held there were fired, preserving them for our reading. Even to this day, more and more records are discovered. One of the most impressive finds, in very recent time, has been a sealed, nine-by-six-foot room in Sippar holding, neatly arranged on shelves, a set of some 400 elaborate clay tablets containing an unbroken record of the history of those ancient times, a sort of time capsule. Again, the evidence is so overwhelming and robust that, if it weren't for those with power enough to suppress, it would have been accepted and our world view changed a century ago or perhaps sooner.

..."Working from the same archaeological discoveries, artifacts, and recovered records as archaeologists and linguists have for two hundred years, Z. Sitchin propounds – proves, in the opinion of the author – that the Anunnaki (Sumerian: "those who came down from the heavens"), an advanced civilization from the tenth planet in our solar system, splashed down in the Persian gulf area around 432,000 years ago, colonized the planet, with the purpose of obtaining large quantities of gold. Some 250,000 years ago the documents tell us their lower echelon miners rebelled against the conditions in the mines and the Anunnaki directorate decided to create a creature to take their place. Enki, their chief scientist, and Ninhursay, their chief medical officer, after getting no satisfactory

Introduction Cont'd (Neil Freer White Paper)

results splicing animal and Homo-Erectus genes, merged their Anunnaki genes with that of Homo-Erectus and produced us, Homo sapiens, a genetically bicameral species, for their purposes as slaves. Because we were a hybrid, we could not procreate. The demand for us as workers became greater and we were genetically manipulated to reproduce.

Eventually, we became so numerous that some of us were expelled from the Anunnaki city centers, gradually spreading over the planet. Having become a stable genetic stock and developing more precociously than, perhaps, the Anunnaki had anticipated, the Anunnaki began to be attracted to humans as sexual partners and children were born of these unions. This was unacceptable to the majority of the Anunnaki high council and it was decided to wipe out the human population through a flood that was predictable when Nibiru, the tenth planet in our solar system and the Anunnaki home planet, came through the inner solar system again (around 12,500 years ago) on one of its periodic 3,600 year returns. Some humans were saved by the action of the Anunnaki, Enki, who was sympathetic to the humans he had originally genetically created. For thousands of years we were their slaves, their workers, their servants, their soldiers in their political battles among themselves. The Anunnaki used us in the construction of their palaces (we retro-project the religious notion of temple on these now), their cities, their mining and refining complexes and their astronomical installations on all continents. They expanded from Mesopotamia to Egypt to India to South and Central America and the stamp of their presence can be found in the farthest reaches of the Planet.

Around 6,000 years ago, probably realizing that they were going to phase off the planet, they began to gradually bring humans to independence. Sumer, a human civilization, amazing in its "sudden" and mature and highly advanced character was set up under their tutelage in Mesopotamia, human kings were inaugurated as go betweens, foremen of the human populations answering to the Anunnaki. Some humans were taught technology, mathematics, astronomy, advanced crafts and the ways of civilized society. The high civilizations of Egypt and Central America arose."*

---

* This concludes my excerpts from Neil Freer's "The Alien Question: An Expanded Perspective – A White Paper'" Posted Wed. 6-Oct. 1999 04:38: 17 GMT. Printed with permission of Neil Freer.

THE EARLIEST CIVILIZATIONS

As written on cuneiform tablets, the ANUNNAKI arrived on Earth in the Persian Gulf many millennia ago. There were no humans on our planet for the first 200,000 years the ANUNNAKI were here. The species, Homo erectus, had been evolving on Earth for over 1,800,000 years. In the beginning the ANUNNAKI had no interest in this primitive nonverbal Homo erectus.

According to Zecharia Sitchin's translations, the ANUNNAKI desperately needed gold to close an ozone leak in the atmosphere of their planet Nibiru. From the evidence of what the ANUNNAKI left on our planet, I conclude their need for gold was the driving force that kept them here for hundreds of thousands of years. In The 12th Planet, Z. Sitchin wrote the ANUNNAKI first attempted to extract gold by the slow process of vacuuming the floor of the Persian Gulf. This process of separating gold from "non-gold" minerals was inefficient. Their first land base was Eridu, which translates from Sumerian into "home in the far away." I assume the ANUNNAKI gradually moved up the Tigris and Euphrates Rivers (today's Iraq) to get closer to the source of gold and established many settlements, such as Nippur, where a Ziggurat was used to extract gold. Below is a map which shows the early ANUNNAKI settlements and the rivers that carried gold from the mountains, of what is today Turkey, to the Persian Gulf. The red dots were the first ANUNNAKI cities before the Great Flood.

Ancient cities of the Anunnaki

- First cities of the gods (Anunnaki)
- Later ancient cities (6000 years after the Great Flood)
  By permission of Z. Sitchin

The Earliest Civilizations (Cont'd)

The map on page 6 (fig.2) shows the approximate time lines of the three oldest recorded Mediterranean civilizations. All three civilizations are dated well *after* the ANUNNAKI first came to our planet. There are time overlaps. The scientific community tends to agree the earliest known human civilization on Earth was Sumerian which dates from 3200 B.C., approximately 5200 years ago.

Mankind's earliest history, which was written in Sumerian on cuneiform tablets, contains an enormous amount of information about this early civilization. To me, this suggests that Sumerian was probably the language spoken by the ANUNNAKI. These tablets contain historical information and thought provoking stories which were undoubtedly orally transmitted for millennia before being written down. History may eventually uncover an earlier start date for the Sumerian civilization and thus possibly for humanity.

Earth's first written story, the "Epic of Gilgamesh," was recorded on 12 cuneiform tablets. On the 11th tablet of this Epic (fig.l) there is a story of a Great Flood that occurred around 11,500-12,500 years ago. Archaeologists confirm there was, in fact, a flood of enormous magnitude around that time, so I suspect that story has validity. This raging flood wiped out the ancient ANUNNAKI cities and devastated large portions of Earth inundating the land with huge deposits of mud.

(1)

My further research has led me to conclude this Great Flood was actually a gigantic 1000 foot high tsunami.

The Earliest Civilizations (Cont'd)

Most all plants, animals and human life forms on the surface of Earth were lost at the time of this flood. Under such harsh destructive conditions human recovery (finding habitable dry land, growing crops, animal domestication, etc.) could have taken as long as 6000 years. For humans to have survived such a calamitous event some "outside" help would seem to have been a necessity. On the 11th tablet of the "Epic of Gilgamesh" it is written that the ANUNNAKI provided domesticated wheat, sheep and other essentials to the survivors of the flood. Evidence of 9000 year old domesticated wheat has been found on the slopes of Mt. Ararat, Turkey.

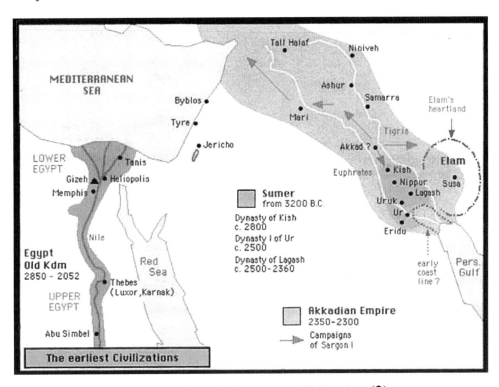

Map of 3 earliest Mediterranean Civilizations (2)

The map above indicates the Egyptian civilization dates from 2850 - 2052 B.C. which equates to 4862-4064 years ago; 350 years *after* the Sumerian civilization. There is archaeological evidence* that the Giza Pyramids were built 10,500 years ago - which is well before the Egyptians were here. This brings into question who built these incredible Egyptian structures while humanity was struggling to recover from the Great Flood? The answer is: The ANUNNAKI were here!

*See time studies of Orion Belt formation and of water erosion on the Giza Sphinx.

MY THEORY

Now that you have some understanding of the lengthy history of the ANUNNAKI, I can divulge my latest discovery - perhaps my most defining moment. I am going to introduce new physical evidence which will illustrate that the ANUNNAKI were intensely involved in the pursuit of gold while they were here for hundreds of thousands of years. I theorize they applied their advanced extraterrestrial intelligence to create an international network of washboard and circular gold mining structures to obtain gold needed to repair their planet's atmosphere. Most of their facilities appear to require the pumping and control of water flow to a structure. Other architectural designs involve water flowing over or through structures. The gold would have been collected when water wasn't present. The pictures in this book demonstrate that Machu Picchu, Ollantaytambo, Palenque, Sacsayhuaman, the Greek Theater at Syracuse, and the Great Pyramid at Giza were "washboard gold mining"* complexes. The evidence presented in this book will prove, without question, that the ANUNNAKI used "washboard gold mining" on a scale never before imagined. There are also pictures of ANUNNAKI circular gold mining complexes at Chaco Canyon, Mesa Verde, Witwatersrand, and Gobekli Tepe. All the circular complexes exhibit similar patterns of 3 foot thick circular walls. I am confident more research will uncover many similar sites around the planet. It is interesting that scientists are studying and uncovering other attributes of and possible uses for monoatomic gold (pure white powder gold). Perhaps the ANUNNAKI had other uses for gold as well.

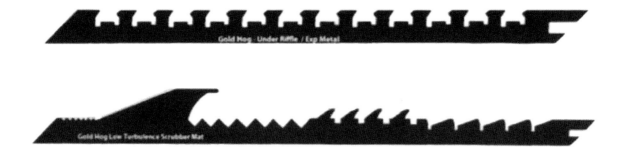

* "Washboard gold mining" is a simple technique of directing river water,
containing placer gold, over a washboard surface allowing the heavy
gold to drop down by gravity onto a collectable surface. Above are
two current designs (Gold Hog) being used today for scrubbing and
extracting gold and heavies from water and sand.

ANCIENT AFRICAN GOLD MINING SITE

Around the same time the ANUNNAKI were building settlements in Sumer they were apparently establishing themselves in South Africa. As is described in the article at http://www.viewzone2.com/adamscalendarx.html, South Africa is the mother lode of gold on planet Earth. The remains of many ancient deep underground gold mines have been discovered in this country over the past 500 years. Recently NASA took this satellite photo (fig. 3) of two of the hundreds of ancient circular stone ruins located at Witwatersrand near Johannesburg, which is also known as "Egoli," which means "city of gold."

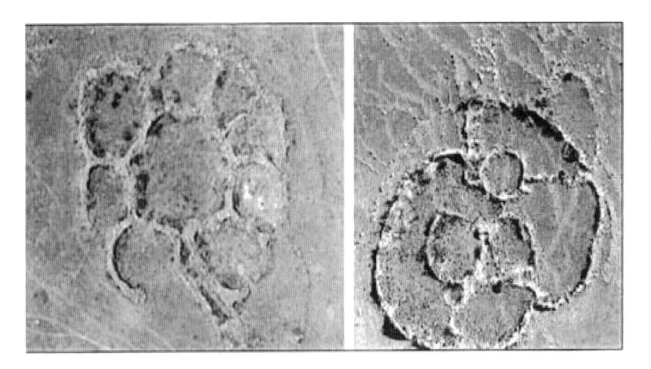

Witwatersrand ruins in Africa (3)

Witwatersrand is part of a 160,000 to 200,000 year old remote metropolis established in the midst of the largest supply of gold in this area. It measures conservatively about 1500 square miles and is part of an even larger complex that covers approximately 10,000 square miles. The surface area pictured above is covered with numerous 3 foot thick circular stone walls. For years local farmers assumed these strange stone formations were built ages ago by indigenous people. Others speculate they were animal corals made by nomadic tribes.

Ancient African Gold Mining Site (Cont'd)

Renowned researcher and author, Michael Tellinger (fig.4), who has spent a great deal of time studying this area, believes "these ruins are the remains of an ancient civilization that lived and dug for gold in this part of the world many thousands of years ago." Tellinger agrees that the ANUNNAKI were the advanced civilization who were operating these African sites. It is difficult to imagine why early Homo sapiens (living 160,000-200,000 years ago) would have spent their time mining gold or had the impetus to build this huge complex. They certainly couldn't eat gold and it was too soft to use for tool or weapon making.

Michael Tellinger in Africa (4)

It would have taken a more highly developed civilization to have constructed this isolated complex. It makes sense that this ancient gold mining complex was not built by the locals. Gobekli Tepe, Mesa Verde, Chaco Canyon, and Sacsayhuaman, which I will be discussing later in this book, all have similar structures to this African site. In Z. Sitchin's translations of the early cuneiform tablets, we are told the ANUNNAKI were mining gold in Africa which chronicles the approximate date of this site. After the Great Flood, which is dated approximately 11,500 to 12,500 years ago, it is written that the ANUNNAKI's underground gold mines were rendered useless (filled with mud) which might explain why we have a significant number of gold mining sites in the New World dated after the Great Flood.

MACHU PICCHU, Peru (Google Elevation Maps)

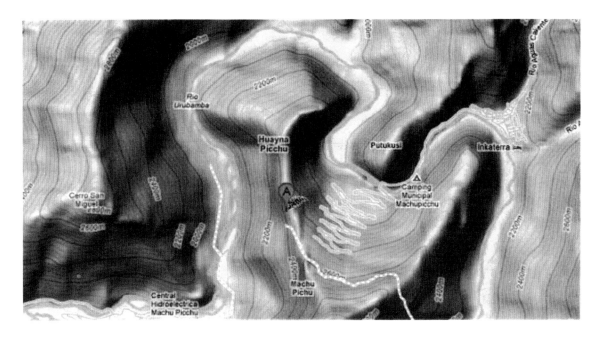

One of the most overwhelmingly massive isolated structures in South America is Machu Picchu (fig. A above). It is located 7979 feet above sea level in the Andes Mountains of Peru. This complex is considered to be a pre-Columbian 15th century Inca site. Most archaeologists believe Machu Picchu was built as an estate for the Inca emperor, Pachacuti (1438-1472). Often referred to as the "Lost City of the Incas," it is perhaps the most familiar icon of the Inca World. On these Google maps you can see that the raging Rio Urubamba loops around one of the granite peaks on which this famous "Inca ruin" was built. In theory, this would have provided its builders two points of access to this gold carrying river; one going north on the right and one going south on the left.

Machu Picchu, Peru (Cont'd)

Often this picture is used to portray Machu Picchu although it only shows a very small portion of the complex. Machu Picchu was declared a Peruvian Historical Sanctuary in 1981, was honored as a UNESC World Heritage Site in 1983 and was voted one of the New Seven Wonders of the World in 2007. It is mind boggling to think a civilization with only primitive stone and bronze tools living high atop a mountain would have had the ability to have built this complex site. I also wonder how and why the Incas acquired such large quantities of gold. On page 30 of my book, <u>ADAM, the Missing Link</u>, there is a similar granite mountain top that was leveled by the ANUNNAKI to provide the foundation for the Giza pyramids in Egypt. And yet, the "scientific community" continues to proclaim the Incas leveled this granite mountain top, constructed all these buildings and built smooth surfaced ashlar* walls.

* Ashlar walls are made of rectangular cuboid blocks of stone that
  are masonry sculpted with square edges and smooth faces.

Machu Picchu, Peru – Entire Complex (Cont'd)

The picture on page 11 was taken from the red dot above in the direction of the red arrow. Missing are the massive sets of cascading terraces pictured above on the left. My conclusion is these multiple sets of descending terraces were in fact part of a washboard gold mining complex. The Urubamba River, rich with placer gold, was directed over these irregular surfaces allowing the heavier gold to drop and settle. The terraces in this picture resemble huge washboards. Presumably the ANUNNAKI had some method for collecting the gold when it came to rest.

I believe they sculpted this granite mountain top because of its unique location in relation to the river. They possibly used the same power beams that leveled the granite foundation under the Great Pyramid at Giza. Pumping river water up 1250 feet to Machu Picchu and directing it to cascade over the terraces shown on the picture above would probably have been a relatively easy task for this advanced extraterrestrial civilization; an efficient way to collect placer gold.

Hundreds of flights of stone stairs, many carved from a single block of granite, run parallel to and through the terraces providing easy access to the deposited gold. There are also numerous channels, mortars and water drains perforated in the solid rock. We know the Incas did not have the proper tools or skills for this type of stonework. Only an advanced civilization could have purposely conceived and executed this massive endeavor!

OLLANTAYTAMBO, Peru

(5)

This site (fig. 5) was built upstream about 40 miles from Machu Picchu. Its massive terraces, built adjacent to the gold bearing Rio Patacancha, offer another example of classic washboard gold mining capability. Could the trapezoidal openings in fig. 6 and enlarged in fig. 7 below, which slant slightly uphill toward the flow of the Rio Patacancha, be possible catchments for gold? Slow flowing water is very cohesive.

(6)   (7)

A nearby site (fig. 8), on page 14, with similar slanted openings, looks like another washboard facility. Two other ancient Peruvian stone complexes (figs. 9 and 10) also appear to have possible "alternative" gold collecting designs. The raised edge (lip) on each terrace could have helped trap gold from the river water.

(8)

(9)

(10)

Raised edge (lip)

CYCLOPEAN WALLS

Cyclopean walls are a significantly larger and heavier type of wall construction than the ashlar walls seen at Machu Picchu and Ollantaytambo. This unique type of wall construction uses massive stones fitted together with minimal, and in some cases, no clearance between them and without mortar. Cyclopean walls appear in many of the ANUNNAKI complexes discussed in this book. Below is a diagram of the cyclopean masonry which acts as the base for the Landing Platform at Baalbek, Lebanon.

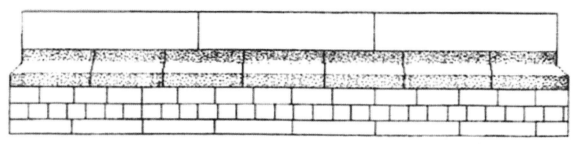

Note the 3 megalithic stones (fig. 11) in the lower left hand corner of this Platform. This structure must have been extremely sacred for the Romans to have built 3 magnificent temples on top of it, 1500 miles from Rome. The largest temple built in the Roman Empire to their god Jupiter is pictured below.

(11)

Cyclopean Walls/Landing Platform at Baalbek (Cont'd)

It is my belief the ANUNNAKI were the builders of the Landing Platform at Baalbek because this type of wall construction would have required extreme precision and workmanship. For example, this massive platform (5,000,000 sq. ft.) was built using four layers of perfectly cut stones (no masonry). The top layer, in the northwest corner, consists of the three largest stones (each weighing approximately 2,000,000 lbs.) ever used in any construction project on our planet. To transport stones weighing 2,000,000 lbs. over one half mile from the quarry and then lift and place them 36 feet above ground level was an engineering task which would be extremely difficult for us to duplicate, even with today's technology. Look again at these three megalithic stones (outlined in red) in figures 11 and 12. The close up picture (fig. 12) of two men standing in the middle of this cyclopean wall accentuates the enormous size of these stones.

(12)

A larger fourth 2,400,000 lb. stone (fig. 13), which continuously receives the most attention, was found abandoned in the quarry. Studying this fourth megalithic stone and considering its proximity to the Platform, makes me wonder if this was an extra stone or could it be the ANUNNAKI intentionally wanted us to see how outrageously skilled they were?

(13)

SACSAYHUAMAN, Peru

Just north of Cuzco, Peru was found one of the most enigmatic stone structures ever discovered in the ancient world. Three parallel stone walls (fig.14) zigzag down a hillside and are constructed with humongous corner stones weighing over 400,000 lbs. This zigzag wall can definitely be classified as cyclopean or megalithic architecture. These walls were built with watertight precision masonry. A razor blade cannot be inserted between the joints. Joseph Davidovitz* found evidence which indicates the Egyptian pyramid casing stones were manufactured. I suggest these watertight zigzag walls could have been produced by a similar process.

Zigzag Walls (14)

Archaeologists speculate this site was built by the Incas as a fortress, a castle or a land made depiction of one or several of the Incas' sacred animals. To date, no other walls with this configuration have been found and no one has declared, with supportive evidence, what their purpose was. Recently many tunnels have been discovered nearby under Cuzco. One is linked to the Temple of the Sun at Koricancha, Cuzco. Koricancha means "courtyard of gold." The Incas occupied this temple for about 300 years before the Spanish. During the Spanish Conquest the temple was looted and 700 sheets of gold estimated to weigh over 3800 lbs., life-size gold figures, solid gold altars and a huge golden sun disc were taken. The Spaniards marveled at the scale of these zigzag walls and could not explain how the native Incas could have built such structures and accumulated such wealth.

* Joseph Davidovits' article: "X-Ray Analysis and X-Ray of Casing Stones...(1984), Published in U.K. pp 511-520.

Sacsayhuaman, Peru (Cont'd)

I too question how this early Inca civilization came into possession of such an enormous amount of gold. If the Incas were not capable of building this site or mining gold, I propose it was designed and abandoned by the ANUNNAKI then later taken over by the Incas. The nearby Urubamba River was gold filled. That might explain why the stones in these zigzag walls were constructed watertight. The picture below shows that these stones fit together as in a jigsaw puzzle.

The 400,000 lb. corner stones were certainly strong enough to withstand the extreme force of any spring runoff from the mountains. If water entered from the right side (of fig. 16) and travelled downhill toward the "exit" (left side of figs. 14 and 16), this would be a *vertical* washboard gold mining complex.

Aerial view (16)

My washboard theory is rotated on its side at this site. I think gold was collected by the zigzag configuration of these walls. When the riverbed seasonally went dry, it would have been easy to walk between the walls or utilize some other extraction technology to retrieve the gold.

TORREON MUYUC MARCA, Sacsayhuaman

(17)

This unusual intricate circular structure (fig. 17), called Torreon Muyuc Marca (TMM), is located <u>uphill</u>, in the same area, less than a quarter of a mile from the infamous zigzag walls.

Could this perfectly circular design, with two visible sluice channels (red arrows above), combined with a possible network of subterranean tunnels between TMM and Qocha* Chincanas, have also been used to separate out placer gold from the Qocha water? In the satellite image on the right, notice that the Qocha Chincanas is on a hilltop at an elevation higher than the nearby zigzag walls.

QOCHA CHINCANAS

ZIGZAG WALLS

TMM

* Qocba" is a lake or pond of natural or artificial origin.

Torreon Muyuc Marca, Sacsayhuaman (Cont'd)

Below is a topographic diagram of Torreon Muyuc Marca (fig.18). The grey lines depict altitude, shown as descending bars, down to the Andean Valley floor. If Qocha Chincanas water was delivered underground to TMM, it could have emerged through the middle of the center ring then cascaded over this ring's edges into the adjacent concentric compartments. A significant amount of gold could have been collected from this ingenious design. Overflow water would have continued downhill toward the zigzag walls over the multiple sets of descending terraces and would have probably joined the annual spring runoff. Additional gold extraction could have then taken place at the corners of the zigzag walls.

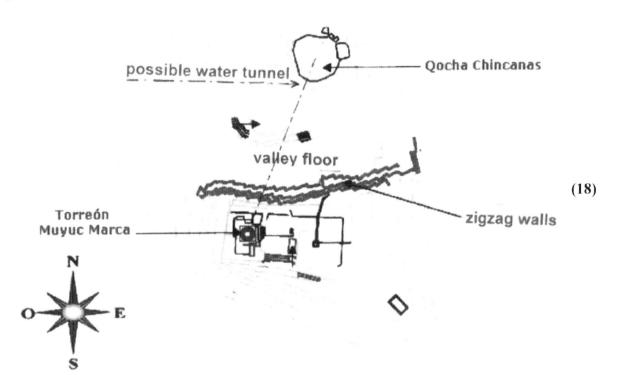

(18)

A hydraulic pulse generator (HPG), or the like, could have been used to transfer water from Qocha Chincanas to TMM. This type of pump requires no outside energy source and was prevalent in the 1700's but lost favor when electrical power became available. To understand how this pump works refer to John Cadman's excellent article at http://scntinelkennels.com/Research_Article_V41.html. I assume the ANNUNAKI were more than capable of transporting or pumping water to or through their gold extraction facilities. The accessibility of large amounts of gold in this valley would have attracted the ANUNNAKI to this location. Their advanced building and technological skills are definitely evident here.

QUETZALCOATL

Many historians and scholars think Quetzalcoatl was a legend. But, the mention of him in so many early cultures leads me to believe he was an ANUNNAKI and the dynamic force behind many of the Mesoamerican cultures. Keep in mind, the ANUNNAKI's life span borders on immortality. In a culture of people who were dark skinned and had no facial hair, Quetzalcoatl would have stood out (fig. 19). He was often described as very tall, fair skinned, long nosed, with beard and having a ruddy complexion; quite different than the physical appearances of the local natives.

Quetzalcoatl=Thoth
Son of Enki
(19)

For generations early Mayan, Inca, Toltec and Aztec civilizations have handed down similar descriptions of him. In Zecharia Sitchin's writings, based on the cuneiform tablets, Quetzalcoatl had numerous names at different times in ancient history. Some of his "also known as" names, throughout his enormously long life, were:

Ningishzidda   - son of ANUNNAKI leader, Enki
Ningishzidda   - builder of the Great Pyramid complex at Giza Egypt
Thoth   - god of Egypt (reigned for 1570 years)
Quetzalcoatl   - builder of pyramids in Mesoamerica (i.e. Chichen Itza, Teotihuacan, Tula,
                   Cholula and perhaps all the other Mesoamerican pyramids)
Quetzalcoatl   - Aztec name
Quetzalcoatl   - Olmec name
K'uk'ulkan   - Mayan name
Viracocha   - Inca name

21.

Quelzalcoatl (Cont'd)

When Thoth (aka Quetzalcoatl) was in Egypt, he was a god-like ruler and a skilled "'keeper of time." This is one of the reasons I credit him with the Calendar Round, referred to today as the Mayan Calendar (fig. 20).

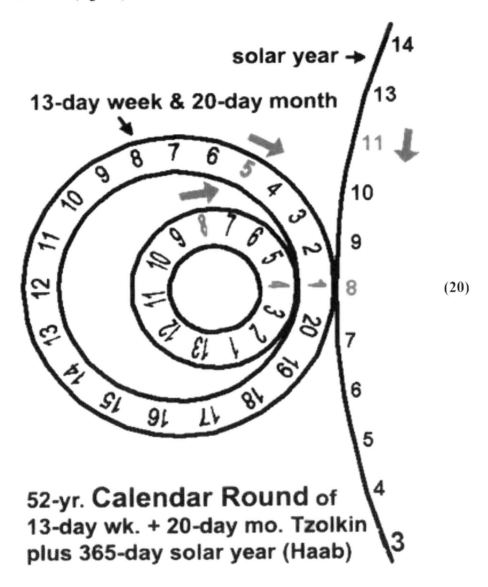

(20)

52-yr. **Calendar Round** of
13-day wk. + 20-day mo. Tzolkin
plus 365-day solar year (Haab)

This "slide rule type" calendar was capable of producing an extremely precise accounting of time for hundreds of thousands of years. The accuracy of this calendar is, in my opinion, an unmistakable sign of advanced intelligence. According to Sitchin, the start date of this calendar was 3113 B.C. The end date, December 22, 2012, is fast approaching. There is considerable speculation about the significance of this end date. In my opinion, it is just the end of another cycle.

Quetzalcoatl (Cont'd)

Quetzalcoatl, a memorable historical figure, was also often symbolized as a feathered serpent by the natives in Central and South America. He was without a doubt brilliant. Quetzalcoatl is credited with introducing culture, the calendar, mathematics, law, metallurgy, astronomy, masonry, agriculture and crafts, as well as, the arts to the New World. This list reads like the "gifts" given the Sumerians by the ANUNNAKI. The one missing "gift," the wheel, which was given to the Sumerians, seems to have been withheld by Quetzalcoatl. I speculate that without the wheel the native human population would have been easier to control.

In addition to advancing Mesoamerican civilization, Quetzalcoatl designed pyramids at Teotihuacan and Giza. There is a three pyramid array pattern at both these sites. Base dimensions of the Teotihuacan Pyramid of the Sun and the Great Pyramid of Giza are very similar. Quetzalcoatl's major New World design change was step construction pyramids with external stairways. The ANUNNAKI often incorporated multiple functions in their projects. For example, the Chichen Itza pyramid produced gold and marked solstices. During the summer and winter solstices, when the sun hit this pyramid's northwestern corner, a slithering snake dramatically appears on the side of the northern stairway (fig. 21). Is it possible Quetzalcoatl put his brand on this site?

The solstice snake (21)

Olmec head (22)

Numerous enormous (10' tall, 25 ton) Olmec head sculptures (fig. 22) have been found in locations throughout Central America. No one has been able to explain why the Olmec people (Africans) were the first recorded civilization in Mesoamerica. It is written when Quetzalcoatl arrived from Egypt he brought tall African helpers with him. It seems logical to me that it could have been Quetzalcoatl who introduced the Olmec people to Mesoamerica.

Mesoamerican Pyramids

Ancient pyramid complexes appear throughout Mesoamerica. Although styles vary, the actual design of most of these pyramids appears to be similar to those done by the ANUNNAKI, Quetzalcoatl, who, according to the cuneiform tablets, is the known architect of the Great Pyramid at Giza Egypt.

GREAT PYRAMID OF CHOLULA, Mexico

The Great Pyramid of Cholula is the largest monument ever built in the world and believed to be the first "step" pyramid built in Mesoamerica. Located in the state of Puebla, this structure was also known as Tlachihualtepetl by the early Aztecs due to its appearance as an "artificial mountain." The excavated site and a diagram of a model of what archaeologists propose this complex once looked like are pictured below (fig.23).

Great Pyramid of Cholnla (23)

Great Pyramid of Cholula (Cont'd)

There are many tunnels under this pyramid but because a lot of the surrounding land is privately owned archaeological exploration has been greatly restricted. As a result, much of its ancient construction history is incomplete. It is thought that the Cholula pyramid was built in the Preclassic Period (about 4000 years ago). If this is true, we should consider "Who were the Native Americans living here who had the technological ability to design and construct this site?" There is evidence that the Olmec, Toltec and Aztec civilizations all utilized this site at different times. Interestingly, ancient Aztecs called it Acholollan, which in Nahuatl means "place of flight" or "water that falls in the place of light." This name has led some, including myself, to suspect the original architect of this pyramid was from elsewhere and/or that water might have flowed down over its outer terraces. Sound familiar?

There are some noticeable differences between this Mesoamerican pyramid and the Great Pyramid at Giza. For one, the base of the big Cholula pyramid is four times the size of the base of the Great Pyramid at Giza. Another significant difference is that the Great Giza Pyramid had a smooth outer wall which makes it a "true" pyramid whereas the Cholula pyramid has a flat top with stepped sides and external stairs which explains why Cholula is described as a step pyramid (See a comparison in fig. 24).

Great Giza Pyramid   **(24)**   **Flat-topped step pyramid, Cholula**

Archaeologists believe the Great Pyramid at Cholula was built in multiple stages. Each stage appears to have a washboard design with horizontal areas for collecting gold if water flowed down from the top. I suspect the ANUNNAKI specifically chose this site for The Great Pyramid of Cholula because there was an ample supply of alluvial gold filled water running directly under this location.

Great Pyramid of Cholula (Cont'd)

In addition to the pyramids in Mesoamerican and Egypt, which I will he discussing in this book, there are other pyramids around the world that should be investigated as possible ANUNNAKI gold mining complexes. It is possible, as we uncover and study all these sites, we will discover and develop new technologies which will advance our own civilization. The red dots on the map below indicate current known locations of other pyramids (fig. 25).

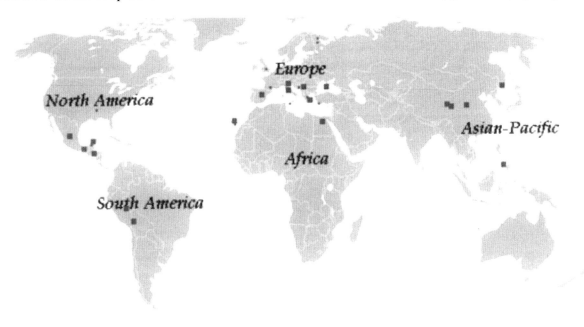

(25) Pyramids throughout the world

PALENQUE, Mexico: Tomb of Pacal the Great

Unlike most other Mayan cities, Palenque (fig. 26), located in the foothills of the Chiapas highlands, enjoyed an abundance of river water. There is evidence of nine separate water sources to be exact, which were controlled by means of a very elaborate aqueduct system. For example, the Otulum River, which runs through the center of this complex, was channeled to flow underneath the floor of Palenque's main plaza using great stone blocks and a nine foot high vault. An important part of this aqueduct featured a pressurized section whose restricted opening could cause the water to exit forcefully, under pressure, which enabled the water to be lifted up to a much greater height. There are numerous step pyramids noted as "Templos" on the site map below in close proximity to the river. If one needs proof of a design which could direct water over washboard surfaces, this aqueduct system would fill the bill.

(26)

Site map

By directing the water from the placer gold filled Otulum River down over the washboard terraces of this magnificent structure (fig. 27), it looks like the ANUNNAKI created another ingenious gold mining facility.

Palenque, Mexico: Tomb of Pacal the Great (Cont'd)

Although only a small amount of this site has been uncovered to date, a cleverly hidden deep underground tomb was found inside the Temple of Inscriptions (fig. 27) by Alberto Ruz Lhuller in 1952. This step pyramid appears to be the only Mexican "Temple" built specifically as a tomb. There is a beautifully carved enigmatic picture on the lid of this tomb's sarcophagus. Scholars think the person carved on the lid was the great Mayan king, Pacal, who ruled Palenque beginning in the year 615 A.D. for 68 years. It is unexplained how this 10 ton lid, let alone the sarcophagus, could have been transported down a narrow stairway to the tomb. Some ancient alien historians, who have examined this lid, say the carved image looks like a space traveler controlling a space ship (fig. 28).

Templo of Inscriptions (27)

Lid of sarcophagus (28)

Careful study of the many other step pyramid structures that complete this Palenque complex speaks volumes to me of the original intended usage of these pyramids and of the original inhabitants of this ancient "Mayan city."

CHICHEN ITZA, Mexico

Many years ago I climbed the stairs on the pyramid at Chichen Itza. It is interesting that each side of this pyramid has a similar stairway with 91 steps. When you add 91 x 4 to the shared step of the top platform, the result is 365. (What a coincidence!) I still have a vivid memory of the difficulty I experienced trying to make the assent. Each step is approximately 12" high and without a handrail I was totally unbalanced. I had to crawl my way up. Descending was even more difficult; I had to sit and bump my way down. This step design would have been more suited to the climbing abilities of the ANUNNAKI who were over 8' tall. Note the protruding stone steps (sets of 3) running up the sidewall of the main stairway. See similar steps on pg. 36. Could these special steps have been used by the ANUNNAKI to access the flat terrace surfaces when collecting gold?

Throughout Chichen Itza's nearly thousand years of known history, the construction of this site has been accredited to the Mayan civilization. True, the Mayans did occupy this site, but that alone does not prove they created it. The astronomical information built into this complex, coupled with the construction technology exhibited in this pyramid's design, confirms for me that this was one of the ANUNNAKI's superb gold mining complexes.

Chichen Itza's Water Supply

Chichen Itza's sacred cenote

This underground water supply (pictured above), located near the pyramid at Chichen Itza, is a natural sinkhole called a cenote. When I visited this site about nineteen years ago, the water was almost up to ground level (top of picture above). This cenote would have been an excellent source of placer water for a washboard type gold mining complex. The large hole, identified by the red arrow above, which is now exposed in this massive underground cavity, intrigues me. What was it for? Could it be that this opening was an intake port used to draw gold bearing water from this underground water source to the top of the pyramid? Alluvial placers are still an important source of gold mining in Mexico and Central America today. Eons of erosion create underground lakes and rivers from which placer gold could have been extracted. If this structure was used for washboard gold mining then it is possible most of the Mesoamerican pyramids, of this design, could also have contributed to the extensive gold accumulating operation of the ANUNNAKI who visited Earth some 432,000 years ago.

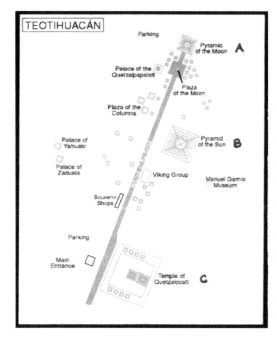

TEOTIHUACAN
"City of the Gods"

This enormous city located near Mexico City was discovered in the 7th century A.D. We do not know when it was originally built. Archaeologists believe the Olmecs lived here first, as early as 3400 years ago. In 300 B.C. it was an ancient Aztec city. It consists of three pyramids with washboard type stone sidings; the Pyramid of the Moon (A), the Pyramid of the Sun (B), the Pyramid of Quetzalcoatl (C) and numerous smaller step pyramids (D). The Pyramid of the Moon (A) is at the end of what has been described as the "Avenue of the Dead". Teotihuacan was one of the largest ancient metropolises in the world.

(A)

(D)

31.

Teotihuacan, "City of the Gods" (Cont'd)

I strongly suspect this site was built by Quetzalcoatl not only because of its extensive washboard type construction but also because the alignment of the three pyramids located here parallels almost exactly the alignment of the Giza pyramids he designed. We know the ANUNNAKI were expert astronomers and space age navigators. It appears to be more than a coincidence that both these pyramid complexes, located on different continents, parallel the Star Belt of Orion.

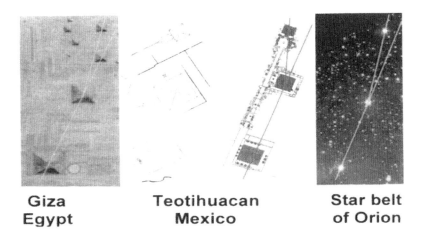

Giza   **Teotihuacan**   **Star belt**
Egypt   **Mexico**   **of Orion**

There is a large deep mysterious hole adjacent to the Pyramid of Quetzalcoatl (E). Could this hole possibly have been a shaft to the water supply for the alien's gold mining operation? The nearby San Juan, San Lorenzo and the Huixlco Rivers would have provided ample water supply to the "City of the Gods."

(E.)

Hole adjacent to Pyramid of Quetzalcoatl

It is unlikely that earlier civilizations who occupied this "city" were sophisticated enough to have built this site by themselves with the tools available at that time. In my analysis, this huge complex of washboard pyramids was another massive gold mining center for the ANUNNAKI.

TULA, City of Quetzalcoatl

Above is a picture of the terraced remains of a pyramidal structure called Tlahuizcalpantecuhtli or Temple of the Morning Star; the central structure in Tula. It is located near the juncture of the Rio Rosas and the Rio Tula in the Mexican state of Hildalgo about 60 miles from Mexico City. The picture below shows the immense size of this complex. Tula covered an area of about five square miles.

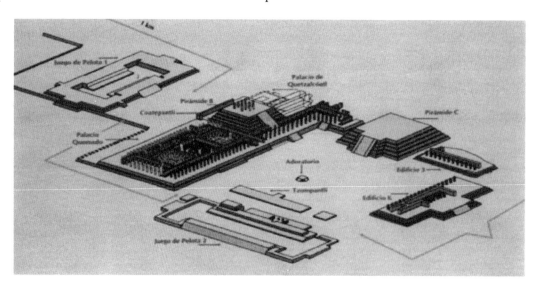

Tula, City of Quetzalcoatl (Cont'd)

It is recorded that Tula was a legendary capital of the Toltec Empire and a thriving metropolis between 900-1250 years ago. The Toltecs are believed to have been the early ancestors of the Aztecs. The name Toltec means "enlightened being" and "artist." Of dozens of sculptured square pillars found here, there supposedly was a pillar sculpted in the form of the feathered serpent Mesoamerian god, Quetzalcoatl, who is thought to have lived here and to have designed this pyramid. Unfortunately, only the legend of that pillar remains and yet Tula is still known as the City of Quetzalcoatl.

Inside this pyramid four 15' tall carved stone statues were found in pieces. At first these statues were labeled "idols." Some thought they were sculpted gods from the legendary city of Atlantis and thus nicknamed them Atlantes. Others said they were simply Toltec warriors. Whoever they were, they now stand assembled, with great honor, on top of the Tula pyramid. What is mystifying is none of the facial features on these statues match any known racial group. There is also a great deal of speculation as to why there is, in the right hand of each statue, a gun-like or torch-like object or tool. See photo below.

Tula, City of Quetzalcoatl (Cont'd)

In 1985 Gerardo Levet, an engineer who Zecharia Sitchin met in Mexico at this site, discovered what looked like a Toltec leader engraved on a Tula pilaster (pictured on the right). In the upper left hand corner, above the leader, is the image of a person holding in his hand what appears to be the very same object as on the Atlantes statues. After seeing this, Levet advanced the theory that this handheld object looked a lot like a flamethrower (yellow) used to shape stone. Levet pointed out that similar Thermo-Jet torches were used in modern times to carve the giant granite dome monument at Georgia's Stone Mountain.*

Engraved pilaster

As more ruble was removed from this Tula pyramid, a precisely sculpted stone pipe, 18" in diameter and made of perfectly fitted tubular sections, was discovered. It ran through the entire pyramid and connected with multiple chambers and canals running underneath this complex. I theorize these elements were part of a system used to pump placer gold Tula River water up to the top of this washboard pyramid which would give credence to this having been a gold mining operation. The possibility of the pump being some kind of a Hydraulic Pulse Generator (HPG) requires more research, but Tula appears to have the necessary components. I agree with Sitchin; these "Atlantean" statues were not of mortal men. They were ancient aliens, the ANUNNAKI, who were here mining gold to repair their planet's atmosphere, or they were some creation by the ANUNNAKI. Wouldn't the flat topped pyramid, labeled "Piramide C" in the lower picture on page 33, have made a convenient landing platform for a whirlwind** to use when transporting gold?

This Tula pyramid is a similar but shorter version of Chichen Itza. Ancient historians think the ANUNNAKI leader, Quetzalcoatl, may have built Tula then left and created Chichen Itza. One noticeable difference between Tula and Chichen Itza is the apparent random protruding stones on all sides of the Tula pyramid. Could this have been another attempt to knock gold out of flowing water?

*Zecharia Sitchin, The Lost Realms (Book IV)
** Marshall Klarfeld, GILGAMESH 10 (pg. 56)

MORAY, Peru

Moray is an isolated archaeological site located upstream from Ollantaytambo and Machu Picchu in the Peruvian Andes at an altitude of 11,500 feet. It is thought to have been an Inca experimental agricultural community but its unique sophisticated design leads me to suspect it was, at one time, another ANUNNAKI washboard gold mining complex. There is a placer gold bearing mountain river which flows from the south right through this site. This river converges downstream with the Urubamba River before it reaches Machu Picchu. Moray consists of several enormous terraced circular depressions. The original purpose of these depressions is uncertain but they could have served as collection areas for gold. The flat protruding stones embedded into the circular walls appear to be a stairway system.

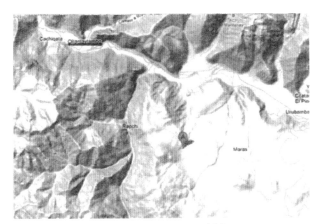

Goggle overview of Moray (A)

Closer view of circular walls at Moray

Terraced circular depressions at Moray

36.

"GREEK THEATER," Syracuse, Sicily

In May 2012 when I visited the "Greek Theater" at Syracuse, Sicily (pictured below), my suspicions were validated. Many archaeologists and historians claim this "amphitheater" was built under the Greek tyrant, Hiero, about 2470 years ago. It was amazingly carved out of a huge solid limestone bedrock hillside. It is extremely difficult for me to visualize hundreds of workers, with primitive iron hand tools, removing thousands of tons of limestone overburden and then accurately carving these multilevel 450 foot diameter semicircular terraces with exact precision. My mind compares this project to the ancient Greeks attempting to create Mount Rushmore. Now I will explain why it was the ANUNNAKI who originally built and operated this site, using technology and tools that we have yet to discover.

Although the theater was being prepped for a performance, I was able to study its core. At first I was attracted to the 6.75 inch vertical wooden steps which led down to the center stage. Underneath these pictured wooden steps I discovered the original 12" high stone steps. Look at fig. 29 on page 38. The average Greek over 2000 years ago, who was probably no taller than 5'2", would have found these initial 12" steps very unbalancing and difficult to climb and/or descend. At 6'2" tall, I had trouble climbing the 12" high steps at Chicken Itza, Mexico. I had to bend over and use my hands going up as there was nothing to grab onto. Coming down I had to sit down and slide over each step. The shorter wooden steps were probably added by the early Greeks when they discovered this site in order to convert it into an amphitheater. If the Greeks

"Greek Theater," Syracuse, Sicily (Cont'd)

had intended humans to use this structure as a "theater" they would have carved more suitable steps that were easier and safer to climb. An eight to nine foot tall ANUNNAKI would not have had any trouble utilizing these 12 inch high steps.

(29)

Next I observed that the horizontal surfaces of these terraces were not FLAT. My photograph (fig. 30) reveals a distinct raised "lip" at the edge of each of these terraces. It is highly improbable that a Greek architect would have intentionally included this "lip" design considering the enormous extra labor required – and for what purpose? The "lip" must have had a special function.

(30)

Raised
Lips

"Greek Theater," Syracuse, Sicily (Cont'd)

Since the ANUNNAKI needed gold, all they would have had to do was harness the Anapos River (Greek for "invisible"), which ran underground at Syracuse, and direct it via aqueducts over the terraces. When the gold filled river water flowed over these lips much of the heavier gold would have been captured by this simple feature. In summary, adding this "lip" design would have been especially useful in washboard gold mining.

The age of this structure cannot be determined since stone cannot be time dated, but the limestone terraces appear to have been subjected to extensive water erosion. I think this was the result of thousands of years of water cascading over these surfaces. I direct your attention, below, to a source of placer water directly above and behind this converted amphitheater. There is water flowing out of a distinctly carved square hole tunnel in the back of a cave. Coincidently, many similar square carved tunnels can be found inside the Great Pyramid at Giza.

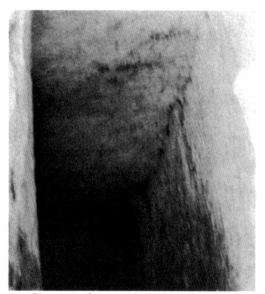

Close up of square hole tunnel

Marshall Klarfeld beside "Greek Theater" water source.

Throughout this book you have read that many ancient structures have been accredited to early local civilizations when in fact, I believe these sites were inherited. This conclusion, that the locals built these sites, is understandable since only recently has the overwhelming proof that the ANUNNAKI visited our planet come to the forefront. From 2008 through 2012, the History Channel (television) has been presenting evidence supporting this in an excellent series called "Ancient Aliens."

TOOLS

Who constructed, in some of Earth's most inaccessible regions, great monuments forged with improbable skills and unknown tools?

One reason I am convinced the ANUNNAKI were here is because the complexes I have examined, some dating as early as 11,000 years ago, would have required a sophisticated understanding of engineering, basic architectural technology and astronomical information. It's unlikely these skills were evident in early humans. Evolution is an extremely slow process. There were no schools or books and it is doubtful early humans were born with this advanced knowledge.

Another reason, and one often misunderstood, is that the tools used by the earliest populations of the world were, by in large, primitive. When you look at the pictures of sites in this book you undoubtedly presume the locals must have had some special construction tools or equipment to have built these elaborate sites. However, that is not a valid assumption. Below are some pictures of the types of tools found by archaeologists. They were primarily made of bronze, wood and/or stone. The Iron Age did not commence until around 1000 B.C. and only in certain parts of the world. Even early weaponry consisted of simple devises such as bows and arrows, knives, and spears. The majority of ancient humans' waking hours were spent obtaining food and protecting themselves, their family and/or their territory. The wheel was never found in ancient Mesoamerica. Construction of many of the ancient sites in this book would have involved years of working with granite, an extremely hard stone. I have uncovered no logical explanation for how large heavy stones were perfectly cut, polished, lifted or moved, at times over difficult terrain and/or great distances, with the mere use of primitive tools.

Examples of ancient hand tools

CHACO CANYON - PUEBLO BONITO

Pueblo Bonito, located in Northwest New Mexico, is the largest structure in the Chaco Canyon complex. The above picture shows an overview of this nearly two acre historical semicircular site purportedly designed and built by the "Anasazi" (which in Navajo translates as ancient ones). There is evidence of erosion from a stream (which probably originated from the gold bearing Colorado plateau) that flowed downhill through the curved "front side" of this site. According to Neil Judd, contracted by National Geographic, this site is an amazing collection of circular depressions carefully crafted using precision masonry with core-and-veneer architecture which produced the massive three foot thick walls and intricate stone work. An example is pictured below. Archaeologists remain baffled at how the early San Juan basin people, who were hunters and gatherers, could have had the advanced technology and construction capability to have built Pueblo Bonito.

Chaco Canyon – Pueblo Bonito (Cont'd)

After studying this site, I suspect this complex was another ANUNNAKI design for extracting gold from water. I was struck by the similarity between the core-and-veneer thick walls here and those seen on page 19 at Sacsayhuaman, Peru.

View from front side of site (31)

The elevated curved front side wall of Pueblo Bonito (fig. 31 above) faces a stream. Why build a wall facing running water with square holes in it? Many of these holes are invisible due to shadowed lighting but there are openings (see two visible holes, lower right in fig. 31) spaced all along this curved outer wall. Then it dawned on me that these square holes were intentionally designed to allow water to enter the complex. The various stone "barriers" and circular interior cavities could have been built to knock down and collect gold as the water passed through the complex.

View from back side of site

The above picture was taken from the flat back side of this semicircular complex and shows two openings that would have been well positioned exits for the flowing water. It appears the ANUNNAKI experimented with or employed multiple designs to extract gold. This site should be studied further in hopes of expanding upon and confirming my assumptions.

MESA VERDE,
Cliff Palace,
Colorado

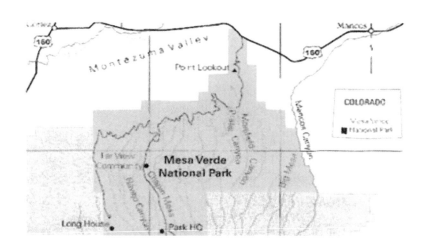

The Cliff Palace (pictured below) is one of many ancient "cliff dwellings" in Mesa Verde. Some of these dwellings are over 5000 feet above the Montezuma Valley and approximately 150 feet below the top of the plateau. Ephemeral streams flowed over this valley for millions of years eroding the softer sandstone layers and producing caves. Water markings are visible on the rocks above this dwelling. Cohesion would have caused water to enter the cave. The

Cliff Palace is right in the path of gold filled water which could have dropped gold onto the floor of this site as water flowed over the cliff and into the cave. Sound familiar? There were people occupying these cliff dwellings in the past who managed with difficulty to provide themselves with the basics. However, I question whether those humans could have constructed these sites. Circular designs are not easily fabricated using stones, mortar, and

Mesa Verde, Colorado (Cont'd)

primitive tools especially when you consider how difficult it would have been to haul all that material up or down these cliffs. More likely most of the Mesa Verde "cliff dwellings" were originally constructed by a significantly more advanced civilization, the ANUNNAKI, and later occupied by the "cliff dwellers." Similar circular gold collection structures appear in Chaco Canyon, New Mexico.

In the picture below you can get a better idea of how gold bearing water (colored in blue) migrated through different levels into numerous collection areas in this site. Perhaps there were ANUNNAKI living in the Cliff Palace supervising the operation which would explain the multilevel structures.

How water could have collected and migrated.

44.

GOBEKLI TEPE, Turkey

This hilltop site, about 1000 feet above a valley, is located in Turkey. When first discovered it was believed to be an abandoned medieval cemetery. As such, it was of little interest to the archaeological community. Then in 1994 Klaus Schmidt, a German archaeologist, visited this site and uncovered what is now being acclaimed one of the most important digs in the world. Schmidt stated that since there was no evidence of people having lived at Gobekli Tepe this must have been a place of worship. Below is an artist's rendition of what one of the many circular structures is thought to have looked like when reconstructed.

Artist's rendition
(reconstructed)

See the two close ups below of some of the circular structures and pillars uncovered at the dig site. Around the globe in Mesa Verde, Colorado (pgs. 43-44) there are remarkably similar circular structures and stonework. Was this accidental or does Gobekli Tepe resemble the makings of another ANUNNAKI gold mining site?

Although only a very small number of these circular structures have been uncovered to date, it has been estimated that these massive limestone pillars are approximately 11,000 years old making Gobekli Tepe the oldest known example of monumental architecture. So far, the scientific community knows nothing of comparable scale that existed on Earth at that ancient time in our history.

Gobekli Tepe, Turkey (Cont'd)

The estimated age of this site is primarily based on some personal artifacts, such as pottery and tools, uncovered at a prehistoric village, approximately 20 miles away. Geneticists also found in that village evidence of the world's oldest domesticated strains of wheat. Radiocarbon dating indicates agriculture developed in this region around 10,500 years ago, five centuries *after* Gobekli Tepe's construction. Needless to say, stones cannot be carbon dated so there is really no way of knowing when this site was built. Nor can the scientific community explain the evidence of domesticated strains of wheat at this early time in Earth's history. Interestingly, in the "Epic of Gilgamesh," it says the ANUNNAKI gave domesticated wheat to humans after the Great Flood.

In National Geographic it was written about Gobekli Tepe that the "T-shaped pillars are thought to be stylized human beings; an idea bolstered by their carved arms with hands reaching toward loincloth-shaped bellies." See the picture below on the left. Pictured below on the right is a massive statue, with its lower portion now exposed. It was recently unearthed on Easter Island; the other side of the Earth. Coincidently, this Easter Island statue has what appears to be an almost identical "hands under belly" sculpted on it. In Chapter 5, of my first book ADAM, the Missing Link, I provide evidence that proves the Easter Island statues were built by the ANUNNAKI.

Gobekli Tepe   **Easter Island (ANUNNAKI branding?)**

I theorize Gobekli Tepe could have originally been another ANUNNAKI circular gold mining complex. It is strategically located near the headwaters of the gold filled Tigris and Eurphrates Rivers. The vertical pillars would have helped knock gold out of placer water as it circulated around inside these multiple ringed structures. I believe there is sufficient evidence to prove this site was originally designed and utilized by the ANUNNAKI.

ZIGGURAT of UR, Nippur, Sumeria

Ancient Sumerian writings on cuneiform tablets (translated by Z. Sitchin) state that the ANUNNAKI left their initial gold separation operations in the Persian Gulf and came ashore establishing the first extraterrestrial settlement in Eridu, which is today in Iraq. Refer back to map on page 4 to view some of their other settlements. It seems logical that the ANUNNAKI would have moved upstream to collect gold from the nearby Tigris and Euphrates rivers which flowed into the Persian Gulf from the gold bearing mountains of what is now Turkey.

Below are a graphic rendition and an aerial photo of the Ziggurat of Ur, located in Nippur upstream from Eridu. Originally only the foundation of this "temple," made of a three layered solid mass of mud brick with burnt brick set in between, was uncovered. The corners of this structure are oriented to the compass points. There have been multiple attempts to restore its original design. To me it is possible that this early pyramidal design, with an outside staircase and terraces, might have been the ANUNNAKI's first attempt at external washboard gold mining.

A graphic of reconstructed Ziggurat at Ur   Aerial photo of restored Ziggurat at Ur

This massive step pyramid, believed to have been part of a temple complex, was thought to have been completed about 4100 years ago by a Sumerian King, Shulgi, who described himself as a "god," the son of Ninsun, and a mighty warrior with exceptional powers and strength. On the Sumerian cuneiform tablets, it was recorded that Ninsun was an ANUNNAKI Queen and also the mother of King Gilgamesh.*

* If you read my 2nd book, GILGAMESH 10, you'll understand why I suspect King Shulgi and Gilgamesb were one and the same.

ANCIENT EGYPTIAN PYRAMIDS

Pyramids have been built in many parts of the world and were for thousands of years the largest structures on Earth. As with most architectural structures, there is an evolution of design over time. The most famous pyramid is the Great Pyramid at Giza and, as such, that will be my focus. There were several early "'attempts" at building pyramids in Egypt that predated Giza. Two of its precursors, the Red Pyramid and the Bent Pyramid, were located in close proximity to the Nile River which flows northward carrying placer gold from the rich Nubian deposits of the Wadi* Allaqli and Wadi Cabgaba.

Bent Pyramid

Red Pyramid

* Wadi is a valley or dried river bed.

Ancient Egyptian Pyramids (Cont'd)

The Red and Bent were the first Egyptian pyramids to contain beautifully crafted internal watertight vaulted chambers and to have smooth-sided pyramidal outer walls rather than the stepped outer walls seen at sites such as the Great Pyramid of Cholula (pg. 24) and Chichen Itza (pg. 29) in Mexico. The Red Pyramid has a single vaulted chamber and the Bent Pyramid has two vaulted chambers.

**Vaulted pyramid chamber
in the Red Pyramid**

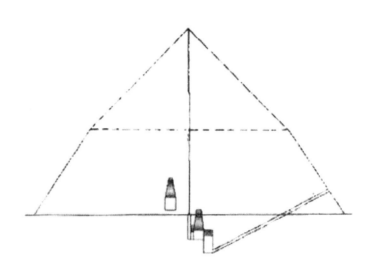

**Diagram showing the internal dimensions and angles of the
Bent Pyramid at Dahshur. (Hassan Mustapha)**

Archaeologists differ in their estimates as to when these two were originally built and for what purpose. It appears to me, from the grandness of the Grand Gallery of the Great Pyramid at Giza, that the Red and Bent pyramids predate Giza.

There is a general consensus that all three pyramids were tombs for Pharaohs although there have never been any hieroglyphs or remains of Pharaohs found inside or, for that matter, inside any of the other Egyptian pyramids. Since these pyramids are located in Egypt, there is a strongly perpetuated belief that they must have been built by local Egyptians. I disagree with this conclusion primarily because all three have huge vaulted granite chambers. Even if an enormous labor force could have been harnessed for many years (a theory I consider doubtful), the obvious, but ignored, stumbling block to that assumption is the early Egyptians lacked tools strong enough to have carved and smoothed these interior stone walls.

THE GREAT PYRAMID AT GIZA, Egypt

When we think of pyramids, we usually envision the Great Pyramid at Giza Egypt. Although many of the shiny outer casing stones have fallen off, the interior structure of intricate passageways and chambers has remained largely intact. For centuries experts have crawled around claiming to have figured out what Giza once was – a Pharaoh's tomb, a power generating machine, a temple to the gods or to the stars, etc., etc. Questions continue but clear answers elude us. To date there is no universal agreement on any of these hypotheses. The fact that the dimensions of its base and the ratio of its height to its perimeter are so precise (and include mathematical formulas, such as pi, and astronomical alignments) baffles the best of the ancient historians and archaeologists who try to explain how and why this pyramid was built. Still many insist this complex pyramid was built by the Egyptians. But, if it was, it has been calculated it could have taken 20 or more years, working day and night, to move and place the estimated 2.3 million blocks of heavy stones and granite. I strongly propose there is significantly more evidence to support this pyramid being built by the space age civilization, the ANUNNAKI.

What has always intrigued me about the Great Pyramid at Giza is the "watertight" construction of the Grand Gallery and the King's Chamber. Interestingly, the Queen's Chamber, the First Ascending Passage, the Horizontal Passage and all of the tunnels from the entrance down to the Descending Passage are also watertight! As an investigative researcher I asked myself "Why did the builders of this magnificent pyramid expend additional time and effort to produce a watertight system?" The answer to that question corroborates my latest discovery.

Watertight King's chamber
(granite stone floor & ceiling)

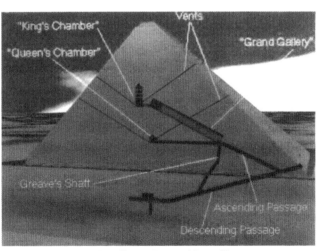

The Great Pyramid at Giza
(internal chambers and passages)

The Great Pyramid at Giza (Cont'd)

Below is a large picture of the Grand Gallery with its unique inward slanted corbelled ceiling and towering watertight granite walls. The two small pictures (fig. 32 and fig. 33) below show interior diagrams and intricate angles incorporated into the architectural design of this pyramid. Not only does this complex design appear to include intellect but purpose as well.

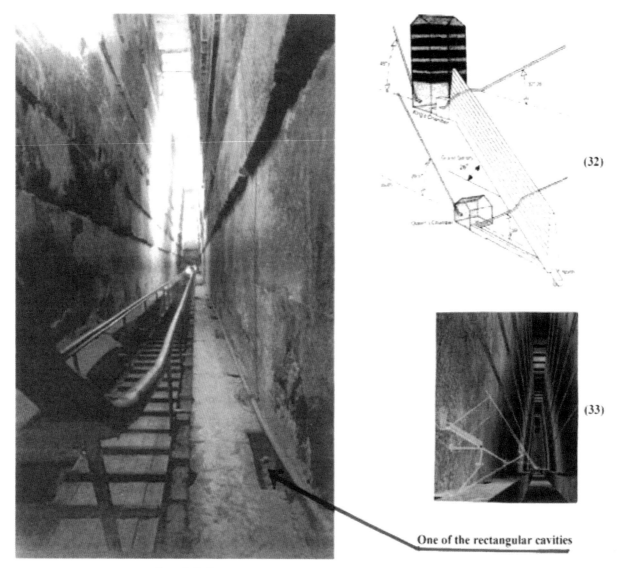

(32)

(33)

One of the rectangular cavities

Grand Gallery

After studying John Cadman's Hydraulic Pulse Generator (HPG) and the work of Edward Kunkel, I understand how it would have been possible to pump Nile River water into the Great Pyramid. That part of their work supports my new theory. Go to http://sentinelkennels.com/research_Article_V41.html to review Cadman's article. The diagram on page 52 (Cadman's article) shows how water from the Nile was available to fill the gap between the pyramid and

The Great Pyramid at Giza (Cont'd)

Location of pyramids in relation to Nile River.

the retaining wall (1-below). Once the water (2-below) height was at the pyramid's entrance, all the dynamic elements of an HPG were available to pump water up into the Grand Gallery. Remember every component of the pyramid's internal structure was designed watertight! The HPG concept was probably used in the Pit. As placer gold water surged up into the Grand Gallery, air channels provided relief from increasing internal air pressure. When this pulsing water made contact with the uniquely inverted washboard configuration (inverted corbelled walls), gold would have been knocked down onto the base of the Gallery and perhaps into the 27 rectangular cavities cut along the sides of the Gallery's downward sloping floor. As the surging water filled the King's Chamber, I believe the "sarcophagus" would float and randomly strike the surrounding surfaces. Damaged edges are visible in picture below.

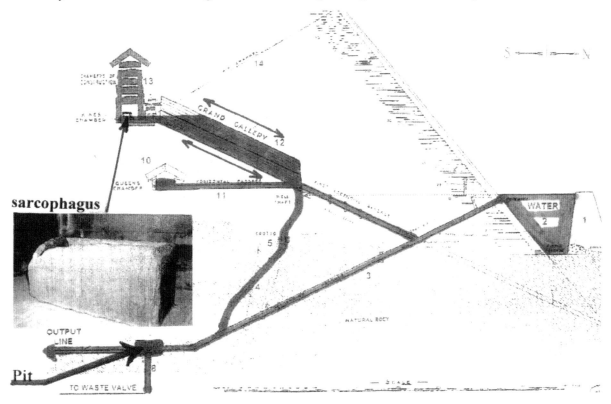

ANUNNAKI BRANDING

It is intriguing how this advanced space age civilization was able to achieve their main goal of collecting gold and, in the same structures, to incorporate celestial signatures i.e. important star alignments, solstice markers and/or beacons for navigation. I suggest this was their way of branding their creations. I wonder if their branding carried an alternative message or purpose. Here are a few examples.

1. The Orion Belt is reproduced in the alignment of the three pyramids at Giza, Egypt and the three pyramids at Teotihuacan, Mexico. Both of these massive pyramid complexes appear to have positioned their two larger pyramids in a straight line with their third pyramid offset mimicking the formation of the Belt of Orion! (pg. 32) I am not surprised that, in recent studies of the Giza pyramid array, it has been determined that the angle of the third pyramid can he traced back in time to match the exact configuration of the Orion Belt 10,500 years ago; a time when the Egyptians did not exist.

2. The Giza pyramids were also reflective beacons used in navigation. (See ADAM, the Missing Link, pg. 29.) They were originally covered with mirror polished casing stones that reflected sunlight to every horizon.

3. The "three window temple" and the "sun temple" at Machu Picchu, Peru have window alignments that track the solstices of the sun.

4. The alignment of the square corners, outside of the perfectly circular construction, Torreon Muyuc Marca at Sacsayhuaman, faces directly toward the compass points of North, South, East and West.

5. The slithering snake, which shines on the side of the staircase of the pyramid during the summer solstice at Chichen Itza, Mexico, was accomplished by careful alignment of this pyramid's base before construction even began. It is doubtful early native populations would have possessed the skills necessary to make this interesting phenomenon a reality.

6. The same reasoning applies to directing the sun to shine through the "door" and down a tunnel at Newgrange, Ireland during the winter solstice. The Newgrange site also doubled as a reflective beacon. 1000 shimmering white quartz stones were built into the roof and the east facing wall of this complex. (Refer to ADAM, the Missing Link, pg. 38.)

ANUNNAKI Branding (Cont'd)

7. The Easter Island statues (fig. 34 below) were assembled on top of an "Inca" ashlar type wall in a desolate location 2000 miles from civilization. All of these statues faced eastward with white coral eyes. Most of the coral stones that originally reflected upward in the morning sun are missing today. After the sun set on the brilliant Giza pyramids in Egypt, these Easter Island statues' eyes lit up. I find it more than curious that the shining beacons of these two distant locations are *exactly* 12 hours apart.

Easter Island Statues (34)

8. There are sculptures depicting a helicopter, a shuttle craft and a "'submarine" on the ceiling beams of two ancient massive temples in Karnak and Abydos, Egypt. It is improbable these 20th century objects would have appeared in a Pharaoh's temple some 3000 years ago.

Branding on Egyptian temples?

Creative types have been branding their work ever since the beginning of time. It is not surprising to uncover identifying signatures prevalent on structures left behind by the ANUNNAKI. There are many other complex structures around the world designed by the ANUNNAKI that require more research before they can be included in my new washboard gold mining theory. However, there is one questionable site that I intentionally mention in this book. It is Puma Pumku. This unique complex intrigues and baffles today's most brilliant historians and archaeologists but definitely has the "fingerprints" of the ANUNNAKI on it.

Tiahuanacu, Bolivia aka PUMA PUMKU

Puma Pumku, adjacent to Lake Titicaca, is a mystery. It is estimated to be "very very" old but no one can agree on its age. This strange scattering of unusually shaped stones, some of megalithic size, has caused a flurry of curiosity among those who have studied the site. What stimulates my interest the most is the overwhelming evidence of incredibly advanced stone cutting technology. Many stone corners are cut at 90 degrees (pictured above/below) with a smoothness and precision that would have been impossible to achieve 1000s of years ago without advanced equipment and/or tools. I believe these stones were made by the ANUNNAKI since they are the only extraterrestrial visitors in ancient history that we have record of to date. By studying the various stone structures, I see some of the makings of a gold separation complex. However, since I am not able to reconstruct this puzzling display of stones to prove that point, I am only including Puma Pumku's enormous intricately formed stones as further evidence that "The ANUNNAKI were here!"

CONCLUSIONS

In my first book, <u>ADAM, the Missing Link</u>, I focused primarily on the physical evidence which supports the existence of the ANUNNAKI. In this book I introduce my new theory that the ANUNNAKI employed washboard gold mining complexes using step pyramids and varieties of circular gold separation structures throughout North, South and Central America, Egypt and Mesopotamia. There are other sites, not shown, such as Carat, Peru, Chavin de Huantar, Peru, and Tenachtitan, Mexico that also exhibit ancient gold mining elements.

If this new theory is correct, it should conclusively prove that not only was an extraterrestrial civilization, the ANUNNAKI, *here* on planet Earth for many thousands of years, but, with time, it could also provide mankind with more insightful information about this alien civilization and its advanced technologies.

I feel it is time for our educational institutions to introduce, at appropriate grade levels, the story of the ANUNNAKI and their influence on our ancient history. The theory of Genetic Engineering, in addition to the theories of Evolution and Intelligent Design, should also be offered at appropriate grade levels. Let the future leaders of our civilization decide for themselves "how it all began."

It is also critical that the international scientific communities and the global leadership of the world acknowledge the reality of the ANUNNAKI's existence, including their enormous influence on humanity. Sharing and investigating a common past could help unite our fragmented world.

POST SCRIPT

Should there be a new time line for ANUNNAKI creations on planet Earth?

The planet Earth is spinning around the North/South axis like a giant top. Our spin rate is declining causing the North Pole to wobble like a spinning top as it slows down. Each time the North Pole settles into a new position a new equator is created. In Jim Alison's report* he did a reverse engineering process wherein he was able to recreate the changing equator location backwards over time. According to his calculations for the period between 120,000 to 84,000 years ago (36,000 year period), the equator was the white line shown in the schematic on page 58. If that equator line is positioned correctly, it clearly shows that the Nazca Lines in Peru, Atlantis (possibly located in the Verde Island group), the Giza Pyramids in Egypt, the Plain of Jars in Laos, Easter Island and Ollantaytambo in Peru (on the same line, but not shown) would all have appeared on that white equator line during that time in ancient history.

It is a known fact that when landing on a planet from outer space it is advantageous to land using the equator as the landing path. Orbiting space craft use the drag at the Earth's equator to help with reentry. The Jet Propulsion Laboratory at CALTECH recently demonstrated this when landing Curiosity at Mars' equator. I believe all of the locations mentioned above could have intentionally been created by the ANUNNAKI as navigational landmarks when they first came to our barren planet. When the sun set on the brilliant Giza Pyramids (formerly covered with shining casing stones), 12 hours away the Easter Island coral eyes lit up (ADAM, the Missing Link, page 36). In daylight hours, Atlantis, with its bronze walls (according to Plato), would have shown as a beacon and the Nazca Lines are visible from space today. If filled with water, the Plain of Jars would also have reflected skyward. My investigative mind asks the question "Would the ANUNNAKI have specifically chosen to create these visible sites as a simple early guidance system on a planet lacking an electronic infrastructure?" And if so, should we now date these multiple locations to at least 84,000 years ago?

* http://home.hiwaay.net/~jalison/

EQUATOR: 120,000 – 84,000 YEARS AGO

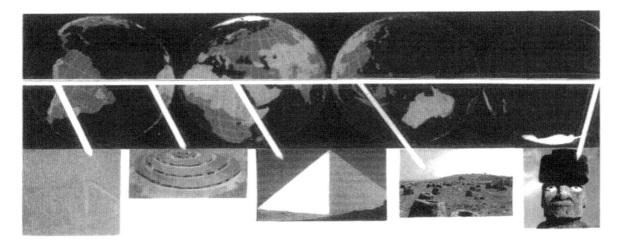

Nazca Lines   Atlantis   Giza Pyramids   Plain of Jars   Easter Island

Made in the USA
Charleston, SC
28 September 2012